ESPRESSO MAKING PERFECTION

MAKE PERFECT ESPRESSO EVERY TIME

ANTONIO VERONA

Antonio Verona

UK

This publication is designed to provide accurate and authoritative information in regard to the subject matter covered. It is sold the understanding that the publisher is not engaged in rendering legal, accounting, or other professional services. If legal advice or other expert assistance is required, the services of a competent professional person should be sought.

First Printing, 2012

ISBN-13: 978-1475110845

ISBN-10: 1475110847

Printed in the United States of America

CONTENTS

INTRODUCTION

Thank you for picking up your copy of Espresso Making Perfection by me, Antonio Verona.

Making perfect espresso is more of an art than an exact science and even after becoming proficient, it can still be hit and miss simply because there are so many variables at play.

However, by following the advice in this guide you'll be able to make perfect espresso, or espresso better than you've ever tasted, the vast majority of the time.

Recent studies have shown that 90% of Starbucks, and other coffee shop baristas, actually have little knowledge in making high quality espresso. By the time you've finished reading this book, you'll be able to teach them a thing or ten. I'm not by any means criticising Starbucks or other coffee shop staff; I'm fully aware that many of them are young and on basic wages, perhaps even working in their first ever job. In any case, there are variables outside the control of coffee shop staff, such as bean quality, which one cannot blame on a minimum wage barista.

Included inside are a range of espresso drink recipes. Espresso is a passion of mine and I really want to pass on the love.

I've been making espresso for thirty years using a range of machines; manual, semi-automatic and fully automatic and so I'll also include a short summary for what I consider the best machines in each category.

Keep in mind that you really don't need to own an expensive machine to make perfect espresso from home, in fact I always recommend starting with a budget machine. You may then invest in a higher quality espresso machine as you progress.

I hope the information you're about to learn is worthwhile and that you'll refer to this book in the future, as and when needed.

THE COFFEE YOU PURCHASE

Being the fundamental ingredient, obviously, this point is of primary importance.

Usually, the options you have are purchasing packets of either beans or grounds. If you don't yet own a grinder then you're likely to purchase grounds, however, to achieve that superior espresso taste, then at some point you'll wish to purchase a grinder to go alongside your espresso machine, at which time you'll progress to buying coffee beans over grounds.

The superiority of beans over grounds is due to one major reason; coffee grounds lose freshness, and therefore flavour, extremely quickly.

The reason for this is that the moment a bean has been ground, the resulting particles, many thousands of them, undergo an exponential increase in surface area. Consequently, these tiny particles are exposed to a far greater level of oxygen and the result is a loss of flavour. This can happen extremely quickly, which is why, in coffee shops, you always see the baristas grind the beans immediately before use. This is why all reputable coffee outlets should sell beans in addition to grounds.

You could even take this principle one step further to keep your beans fresher for longer by purchasing beans in their pre-roasted state.

Is this possible? Why, yes, as long as you order from a specialist. What are the advantages? Let me explain.

When coffee beans are picked at source, they are cleaned before being shipped abroad. They are then received in their green and un-roasted state and your supplier, or coffee shop or chain, then carry out the roasting themselves. Why do they do this? Because the moment a coffee bean has undergone the roasting process the inevitable decomposing begins. Let's take Costa Coffee as an example, who create their unique blend from a mixture of beans from Brazil, Columbia, Ethiopia and Vietnam. By roasting their beans at their roastery in London, they do all they can to guarantee the shortest possible time between being roasted and arriving at their many stores, ensuring the beans are in their freshest and highest-quality state when reaching the end consumer. However, it can still be many weeks after roasting when any particular batch of coffee is finally used, and it doesn't take a coffee connoisseur to notice the often inconsistent quality at most coffee chains from one day to the next.

Let me reiterate; after roasting, decomposition begins, however, beans in their green, un-roasted state can last for quite some time.

How can you get round this? Check if your supplier roasts

beans to order! Imagine going to your local specialist roaster and being handed a bag full of beans that are still hot in the bag. This is what you should be aiming to buy.

Alternatively, and for the more advanced espresso enthusiasts, you may wish to purchase your very own roasting machine for the home. By then purchasing green, un-roasted beans, and roasting them yourself, you're removing that one major element that contributes greatest to loss of freshness and flavour. This makes a huge difference to the overall taste.

Roasting ovens are freely available on Amazon and, of course, come at a variety of price points and so any purchase made should depend on the level you're at. However, I'll point out that in order of importance, spending money on a roaster should come third behind an espresso machine and a quality grinder.

USE QUALITY BEANS

This next espresso making tip is also very important.

Using a salad analogy; if you're intending on making a quality salad, one to impress your friends and family, then you wouldn't go about it by pulling out-of-date ingredients from a dumpster behind a supermarket. No, you'd purchase only the freshest tomatoes, lettuce and everything else that goes with it. A quality salad, just like quality coffee, starts with having quality ingredients.

It always surprises me just how many people attempt to make espresso at home with beans of low quality; either old beans or beans from one of the poorer coffee growing regions.

Now might be a good time to say there's no such thing as an espresso bean. Espresso beans are the exact same as coffee beans. The difference between the two drinks is in the grind and the process of making it, which of course we'll get into.

So what kind of beans should you purchase?

Well, if you purchase your beans from a local superstore then you should be looking at the grading on the packet. The higher the grading the better quality of bean in the pack.

Keep in mind, however, you're never going to get truly great beans from your local Walmart or Tesco.

To get the truly great beans, you need to go to the specialist places that order straight from source, and what's more, a source that's known to produce quality.

Where are the best sources for coffee beans? I'm going to stick my neck out and say the best sources are the mountainous regions of Central America. I'm talking Honduras, Nicaragua, Costa Rica and of course the very best beans in the world, Panama, whose beans routinely win the Rainforest Alliance, as well as the Speciality Coffee Association of America Roasters Guild, and numerous other awards.

Coffee always tastes better when grown in mountainous regions, such as these places, because they grow a lot slower in these environments. The beans of Panama are known to be the very best in the world, which will enable a superior espresso taste, though of course, you'll pay a premium for these beans.

Jumping from Panama to your home town; find out where your local specialist store is and purchase beans from there rather than the local soulless Walmart. If you don't have a local specialist or you'd like to try something different then there are specialist online shops you can order from. Try:

http://counterculturecoffee.com

Counter Culture is a world famous coffee roaster who've pioneered the "third wave" coffee movement. They're ethical traders who like to look after their farmers and you may even be able to get some elusive beans from Panama too. Unfortunately, at this moment, Counter Culture only ships to the US and Canada.

If you're in the UK, simply carry out a web search for "UK coffee roasters." I actually recommend:

http://www.origincoffee.co.uk/

Origin Coffee is another ethical trader who build lasting relationships with their producers at source.

I have no affiliation to either of these coffee roasters; I recommend them purely on their first-rate reputation.

TYPES OF BEANS

There are two types of coffee bean; Arabica and Robusta.

Arabica is grown at high altitudes in both the eastern and western hemispheres, whereas Robusta is grown at low altitude in the east.

Robusta tends to be a lot stronger than Arabica, which tends to be more flavoursome than Robusta.

Generally, Arabica is used in espresso due to its superior taste and quality. Robusta, because of its lower quality, tends to be found in jars of instant coffee, which you find in the supermarket.

Many speciality coffee shops and roasters will place between 5 – 15% Robusta in their espresso blends in order to add that kick. The added Robusta also gives a superior layer of crema to the espresso. Keep your eye on this ratio as your preferred concentration of Robusta, whether zero or beyond fifteen percent is something that will be personal to each of us.

If making your own blends then my suggestion would be to begin by using 100% Arabica beans and then gradually phasing in Robusta in small increments until finding a ratio that suits your palate. How I do it is by using weighing scales, finding the weight of my bag of Arabica and then, having settled on a ratio of ten percent, will measure the Robusta and mix those beans in with the Arabica.

Trial and error. Everybody's taste is different.

GRIND YOUR OWN BEANS

There's a saying in the espresso business that goes "your grinder should be twice as expensive as your espresso machine."

This is true and I'll tell you why.

You can easily make perfect espresso with a good grinder and a cheap espresso machine, but it's next to impossible to make high quality espresso with an expensive espresso machine but with a cheap grinder.

The quality is all in the grind.

And that is the reason people spend hundreds of dollars on high quality espresso machines, hand built in Italy and then wonder why their espresso tastes worse than down at the local Starbucks.

When starting out making espresso from home, you should first invest in a quality grinder and then progress to a quality espresso machine. Remember that the difference between making a coffee and making an espresso is all in the fineness of the grind.

So what type of grinder should you go for? If you take a little look on Amazon.com you'll find there are many types of grinders.

Grinders come in two main categories; blade grinders and burr grinders.

Blade grinders are ideal for grinding for coffee, however, when making espresso, you really need a grind consistency or you'll have problems when pulling your shot. This is why I recommend going with a burr grinder. Burrs are far more capable of achieving a superb consistency of grind without heating the grinds, which would impair the taste and what's more, they do all this very quickly. Burr grinders can be loud, I'm sure we've heard them at the coffee shop, but I'm afraid it's something you'll just have to live with.

The best burr grinders allow the user to carefully select a precise fineness of grind, another thing that's personal to each aficionado. In edition to an espresso grind, a burr grinder should also allow an option for filter coffee, all the way down to the most finely ground Turkish coffee.

The grinder I recommend is the Baratza Vario.

The Vario uses ceramic burrs as opposed to stainless steel burrs. Ceramic burrs don't heat up while grinding, the consistency is second to none also. The other advantage this machine has over its rivals is that it has a stepless design. This means that changing settings is a simple matter of using a lever as opposed to turning the bean hopper itself, which can be awkward, and is a design which all too many grinders tend to have. However, the main reason for buying the Vario comes down to how closely you can get the grind to the perfect fineness or texture. It has 230 grind settings compared to the 55 of its nearest rival.

This is the grinder I've been using myself for many years without any problems. I highly recommend it.

Whichever machine you go for however, please keep in mind that you'll ideally need to replace your burrs at least every year. Ceramic burrs typically last around 50% longer than steel burrs, another advantage to the Vario.

You should also know that some grinders are specific to certain espresso machines, which means that certain grinders will only accept certain portafilters. The Vario however has adjustable brackets to allow for any shaped portafilter.

Many grinders also come with a doser included. Dosers are what the grinds drop into after grinding and you typically pull a lever to release the grinds into your portafilter (you may have seen them in your local coffee shop). The advantage of having a doser is that you don't need to stand there holding your portafilter while you wait for the machine to grind, you simply pull the lever and the grounds are released. This makes everything faster, which is another benefit if you frequently entertain large numbers of guests and they will all be wanting one of your quality espressos. However, the down side of a grinder with a doser is that if you don't use it frequently, you can have your grinds resting in the doser for a long period of time which, of course, will cause the grinds to go stale. In addition, if you're entertaining without a doser, you could have a long wait to have a dose ready for all your guests. As always, the model which will be best for you will depend on your precise intended usage patterns.

STORING YOUR BEANS AND GRINDS

Ideally you'll be storing espresso beans and not grinds. However, this is not always possible, especially if you don't yet own a grinder. The best scenario would to grind your beans immediately prior to use in order to ensure maximum freshness and flavour.

No matter what you do though, it's always best to purchase beans in small quantities. This will help ensure they're not lying around in the home for too long losing freshness.

Many bean packs possess special sealers to close the bag. However, it's far better using an air tight and sealed container kept stored in a cool dark cupboard. A simple plastic tub is all it takes.

There's much disagreement, and you will read in many places too, that it's suggested to keep your beans or grinds stored in the refrigerator. Indeed, I've been amazed at how many of my friends do just this, however, not myself. Sure, it will keep them fresher for that little bit longer, as this is what the refrigerator is for, alas, wouldn't it be better simply to purchase your stock in smaller quantities and at more regular intervals, bypassing the refrigerator entirely?

I've even known some people to keep their beans in the freezer but having developed a seasoned palate over the years, I've found this truly impairs the taste and you too will easily be able to tell which beans have been frozen and which have come straight from the roaster.

USE FILTERED WATER

The reason we use filtered water to make perfect espresso is twofold.

Firstly, as we know, the amount of espresso pulled from a single dose is miniscule. The quality of the water used will be a major determinant of the end taste. Using filtered over regular tap will ensure an espresso outcome of superior quality. This comes back to my salad analogy; always use quality ingredients.

The second reason is for the longevity of your machine and for long term espresso quality. When we filter our water, we remove the majority of impurities. These impurities cause limescale build up over a period of time. Limescale in your espresso machine affects the quality of your end product.

I recommend using limescale remover on your machine at least once a year regardless but using filtered water from the outset will ensure you'll never have to do it any more than that.

KEEPING YOUR EQUIPMENT CLEAN

This is really quite obvious and I'm sure you've noticed your Barista cleaning the equipment after every use. This is important for making espresso, since the quantity received is so small, even the faintest amount of contaminant can have a huge negative impact on taste.

It's also important to flush out your machine after every use. This usually just involves the turn of a lever or dial and is very easy to do. Imagine not doing this and then returning to your machine after several days or longer, there could well be a resultant build up of espresso or hardened milk in the tubes, potentially festering for days or longer. What's going to be the first thing to land in your cup the next time you come to use the machine? Yuck!

Since most are made from plastic, it's good practice to empty the water reservoir after every espresso making session. If leaving water in the tank for an extended period of time then it may come to suffer from a build up of bacteria. I'm sure you're able to tell the difference between fresh water and water that's been left out for a period of time, particularly water that's been in contact with plastic. Of course, this will negatively affect the result of your espresso and trust me, you'll be able to tell the difference. There's no point in filtering the water if you're only going to consume chemicals from the plastic instead.

I suggest regularly cleaning the detachable parts of your coffee machine. However, it's important not to use regular washing up liquid or dish detergent because that stuff is designed to break down oils. Since much of the desirable taste from espresso is in fact *oil* you'll only end up impairing the taste. What I instead recommend is purchasing a specialist coffee detergent. I use products from a company called Urnex, which you can find on Amazon, however there are also quality coffee detergents from PuroCaf and Cafiza. Simply add some coffee detergent to hot water in the washing up bowl and thoroughly scrub away. You can also use these detergents to carry out a back flush of your espresso machine.

In addition to all of this, you should also descale your boiler at least once a year. As you may already know, calcium tends to build up and in addition to impairing the taste of your espresso, it can also damage your machine. The above companies also supply descaling packets. Please also ensure to flush your machine through with hot water a few times before making espresso following a descaling.

PREHEATING ESPRESSO CUPS

By now I'm sure you're beginning to tell there is more to making perfect espresso than you thought and this little thing really does make a big difference.

It would be a shame to get everything right up to this point and then ruin your espresso simply because you failed to preheat the cups. Remember that you only receive a small quantity of espresso, so as soon as the precious liquid hits a cold cup it will have an immediate impact temperature. You can lose ten degrees of heat in one second if you're not careful and then you can't sit back and relax while you drink it, instead you'll be in a hurry to down it before it gets cold.

Some espresso machines, though mostly the larger ones, come with a built-in cup warmer resting on the top. Automatic espresso machines, not my particular favourite, also tend to possess cup warmers, so don't worry if your machine doesn't have one because there's a simple way of preheating an espresso cup that's been left at room temperature. Simply boil some water and pour a small quantity into your cup prior to brewing. Five to ten seconds is all it really takes to heat the cup and you can pour the water away right before beginning the brewing process. Similarly, you can of course use the hot water tap for a similar result.

Can you use the espresso machine steam wand to heat your cup? This depends. Check if your machine uses a single or double boiler. If it uses a single boiler then you could well be decreasing the temperature of the water when you press the button to commence brewing. The result will be a bitter espresso for you. You can however easily side step this issue, simply by waiting for the machine to re-boil. If you have a machine with a double boiler, then one of those boilers will be reserved for the steam wand. The water (or steam) which comes from this boiler is typically heated to a higher degree (hence the steam) and your espresso will not be effected since you won't be using water which comes from that boiler.

Preheating your cup is important yet easy and effective. You will note when standing in the queue at Starbucks that most baristas don't bother preheating the cups.

It may also be advantageous to preheat your brew group (portafilter and group head) if using a semi-automatic machine. There's much cold steel right there, which will cool that freshly boiled water down fast if not preheated. Of course, if making espresso for a group of friends, then it will only be necessary to heat the brew group for the first shot. To heat the brew group, simply run hot water through the machine and catch it in a mug. Easy!

TAMPING

Ok, we're getting close to the fun part now.

Tamping refers to manually compressing the grounds within the portafilter.

This is a step you won't need to do if using an automatic machine, however, in the vast majority of cases, you'll be using a semi-automatic espresso machine and will therefore need to compress the grounds into the portafilter using a tamper.

Most machines come with tampers included in the box, however, it never fails to amaze me just how low quality they nearly always are, even with some of the most expensive espresso machines on the market, almost always being made from cheap plastic. Some machines come with tampers fixed to the side of the machine, which is really bad because it doesn't allow for much manoeuvrability. You will note in coffee shops that the tampers are almost always fixed to the side of the grinder, which means that there's little chance of the barista having any idea of how much pressure is being applied. From my observations over the years, there is nary a barista who I've witnessed applying a sufficient quantity of pressure against the tamper, simply by lifting the mound of grinds against it, to compress them enough to achieve an optimum taste. I have seen exceptions, but by and large tamping is not carried out to a high enough standard in the majority of coffee shops. In my opinion, tamping is something for which both hands are required, in order to get a dextrous feel for the pressure being applied.

Do yourself a favour and go to your local supplier, or purchase a high quality stainless steel tamper online.

The espresso grounds are tamped into the portafilter in order to compress them. This ensures hot water will flow through in an even manner to extract maximum flavour.

Tamping is quite easy to do badly, in which case you'll end up with a poor espresso. If the tamp is too hard, the water will struggle to find an even flow through the portafilter and it will instead eventually find a path of least resistance, some corner of the capsule that's received slightly less pressure, and will thus leave most of the grounds untouched. The result will be a bitter espresso.

If you don't tamp hard enough then the outcome will be too much of an easy flow through the grounds, with the espresso arriving in the cup far too quickly having not extracted the flavour. The result will be a weak and bitter espresso. This is not what you want either.

However, by using the correct amount of pressure, with firm and even tamping, then the water should spread evenly amongst all the grounds within the portafilter and full and maximum flavour will be extracted. The result will be a perfect espresso!

Tamping is one of those things that requires a little bit of practice to get perfect, so while new to the art of espresso making, my advice would be not to use your expensive Panamanian Hacienda la Esmeralda beans but to instead earn your wings with regular budget beans you won't cry over if wasted.

Luckily, learning good technique is fairly easy and once mastered, you won't forget how to do it. To obtain the perfect tamping technique, follow these steps:

- 1. Using your burr grinder to fill the portafilter, even out the dose using a finger. By not ensuring the dose is level, there's a risk of having an unbalanced portafilter, where one side is more compact than other areas, which will cause an uneven distribution of water.
- 2. Apply the tamper to the portafilter straight on, without an angle. You need the pressure to be applied evenly to the entire surface. Many tampers come slightly smaller than the overall area of the portafilter. In this case, simply tamp North, South, East and West, twisting each time you move. The pressure should be even throughout, at 30 pounds. Practice achieving a consistent 30 pounds of pressure with your arm on a bathroom scale, as this is the magic number that makes all the difference. Practice this as many times as necessary in order to consistently achieve this number. It shouldn't take long and once done, you'll have it for life.
- 3. Inspect your work. Everything should be nice

and even. If not then no problem, simply knock the grinds out and attempt again.

- 4. After brewing your espresso, inspect your work again. Knock the grounds out onto a plate. In the worst case scenario, the waste will drip out like sludge, which means not enough pressure was applied. If done correctly, it should fall out in a single block, or cake. Calve it down the middle and inspect for channels where the water cut through. Any visible channel is a sign that improvements need to be made because the water found an easy path through rather than thoroughly immersing the portafilter contents. If not perfect immediately, don't take it to heart, you'll get there after a few more attempts. If the grounds come out as a solid cake with no signs of channeling then your preparation and tamping was probably perfect.

BREWING

This part may differ slightly depending on what machine you're using. But in the majority of cases, you'll simply need to secure your portafilter within the group head mechanism.

For semi-automatic machines, you simply press a button and the machine does the rest.

You'll hear the machine brewing and hopefully there'll be a few seconds pause, which means the water is finding its way around the tightly packed filter, before the espresso begins to flow.

Your espresso should start to filter through after around 5 seconds. After 15 seconds of brewing, a small layer of crema should appear visible on top.

Around the 25 - 30 second mark, you'll notice a slight change in pitch. This means the majority of the tasty espresso goodness has been extracted and after that point, the flow becomes gradually more bitter, so you should press the stop button.

As well as a change of pitch, look out for bubbles appearing, as this is a sign the best part of the espresso has been extracted and you'll be getting only bitterness from now. Most often bubbles and a change in pitch appear simultaneously.

That's it!

Your finished espresso should ideally weigh 1.5 ounces. All you need to do now is sit back and enjoy your reward.

Of course, you may wish to make a latte, cappuccino or Americano, in which case:

Latte = Espresso + Hot Milk

Cappuccino = Espresso + Frothed Milk

Americano = Espresso + Steamed Water

SUMMARY OF ESPRESSO MACHINES

As mentioned earlier, there are three main types of espresso machine; automatic, semi-automatic and manual.

AUTOMATIC ESPRESSO MACHINES

These are the easy to use, push button machines which tend to be on the expensive side. Many come with their own burr grinders inside, so you can see this as a money saver in the long run.

The benefits of an automatic machine is that they're fast and cleaning is minuscule, however, much of the skill and pleasure in making drinks has been taken away.

If this type of machine sounds like your ideal then Gaggia has a range of impressive machines.

SEMI-AUTOMATIC ESPRESSO MACHINES

These come in two main varieties. First, you have the pod or capsule based machine, which are typically popular in office environments and waiting rooms. Unfortunately, they take even more of the skill away than automatic machines and the quality of the espresso is never anything compared to other methods. They're ideal for busy individuals and there's very little cleaning required. However, the cost per espresso is much more expensive using pods or capsules since there's usually a third party company involved in manufacturing the pods and, of course, they need to make a profit too. There's also the danger of the machines becoming obsolete and the capsules no longer being available.

I'm sure you've heard of Tassimo and Nespresso. The Gaggia For Illy Espresso Machine is also one worth considering.

However, my hunch is that good people reading this book will hardly be the types on the lookout for machines that remove the work, skill and love from the process, which brings us to the alternative machines.

The other type of semi-automatic machine is the one we all envisage where a portafilter is filled with espresso and affixed into a group head mechanism. Yes, there's work involved, but the machine does its part of the work too. Once good form is achieved then the quality of espresso achieved from these machines is exceptional as well as consistent.

At time of writing, my favourite semi-automatic machine is the Gaggia 14101 Classic, although some hardened espresso veterans will disagree with my choice and may prefer the Rancilio Silvia. Either way, they're both fine machines and would make a great addition to any kitchen counter top.

MANUAL ESPRESSO MACHINES

Finally we have the manual espresso machine. Although these beautiful works of art, often hand-built, were popular back in the day, they're in fact a rarity these days, which you might only find used in very high end hotels, or as display pieces in Victorian history museums, which is a pity because, if mastered, they're perhaps capable of producing the very best of espresso.

An Amazon search brings up only a very limited choice, with much of the page actually, and incorrectly, containing semi-automatic machines. Unfortunately, progress left manual machines behind, perhaps because there truly is a steep learning curve to become proficient in their use.

Manual machines involve the extra step of pulling a lever to pump water through the portafilter, adding the additional variables of pressure and speed of pull to the process, both of which will have an effect on the overall quality of the espresso. This makes for an exceptionally inconsistent end product.

Getting everything perfect can take time, effort and a lot of wasted grounds, however when you finally hit the sweet spot, there'll not be an espresso on earth to compare.

I've owned the La Pavoni Professional PBB16 Espresso Machine for over twenty years and if I wanted I could sell it for more than what I bought it for. Oh, and just so you know, I've never had a single issue with it, it's probably the best money I've ever spent.

AN ALTERNATIVE

THE STOVE TOP DEVICE

The stove top espresso maker, otherwise known as the Moka pot is a viable alternative and one where you can still make wonderful quality espresso without much of the hoopla involved with using one of the above machines.

I'm going to need to clarify here, that technically the water needs to be pushed through the grounds with at least 9 bars of pressure for the result to be called "espresso." Moka pots will typically force the water through at only around 1 bar. So technically you couldn't sell the result and call it "espresso." It is however "espresso style" coffee.

If you're still on the fence about forking out for what can be a considerable sum for an espresso machine then this could well be an option until you wish to progress to something like a semi-automatic machine.

You can purchase Moka pots from around the $20 mark and so you may wish to own one anyway since they can be great fun. And yes, $20 can get you a high quality Moka pot.

I'll mention right now that Moka pots are ideal for camping trips. I will also confirm that yes, it's true, every household in Italy has one.

How Moka Pots Work

1. Fill the lower section (boiler) with water.
2. Insert metal filter into position on top of boiler.
3. Fill the filter with espresso grounds.
4. Screw the upper section (collecting chamber) on to the lower section.
5. Place on stove.
6. The heat boils the water and steam is created, which in turn rises through the grounds in the filter.
7. Espresso is created which collects in the collecting chamber.
8. When water in the boiling chamber is low, you'll hear the gurgling sound from the Moka pot.

Pros

1. Much cheaper than any other espresso machine.
2. No tamping involved, which removes a quality variable.
3. Easy for beginners.

4. Tastes great.

Cons

1. Quality may not be as high as with other machines.
2. Not technically "espresso."

Tips

1. Don't pack your grounds too tightly or you'll have a long wait for your espresso.
2. Slight risk of explosion on the cheaper or older machines. Always buy an aluminium Moka pot.
3. When new, or when not used for a while, you should make a dry run of espresso, or simply use instant coffee to flush out the factory taste.
4. Purchase the smallest model you can tolerate depending on how many people you'll typically be making espresso for. The smaller pots are known to make superior quality espresso.
5. Enjoy.

STEAMING MILK

Even if latte, cappuccino, flat white, or any milk based coffee drink is not your thing, it's always handy to know how best to make them; your machine is likely to possess a wand, after all, and your guest may well prefer a latte to the more acquired taste of espresso. Knowing how to properly steam milk and create "microfoam" or "macrofoam," rather than simply "frothed milk" will make all the difference to the outcome.

Just as making great espresso takes practice, so does steaming milk to consistently create the perfect texture for any given drink.

Indeed, for creating the required milk for a latte or flat white, you may simply opt for microwaving the milk before pouring the espresso into the cup. This will still create a delicious end result. However, this book is titled *Espresso Making Perfection* and so we're aiming for more than just delicious. Indeed, if you're entertaining or would like to make use of the milk frother or steamer attached to your machine then you'll very well wish to create that perfect microfoam for your latte.

The kind of foam you should aim to create will depend on the drink you're making. Depending on how you create the foam, the consistency will range from between thick and bubbly (macrofoam) for cappuccino all the way to a more pure hot liquid with tiny bubbles (microfoam) for lattes and flat whites. For the rest of this section I'll refer to the foam as either macrofoam or microfoam respectively for cappuccino or latte.

Microfoam is distinct to a more frothy texture (macrofoam) because microfoam consists of tiny bubbles, barely distinguishable from hot milk. It should shine and have a velvety appearance. On the other hand, macrofoam is more dull, resembles heavily beaten egg whites and is quite thick, ideal for cappuccinos. It is this texture you'll frequently see inexperienced baristas creating for your latte when it would in fact be more suited to a cappuccino.

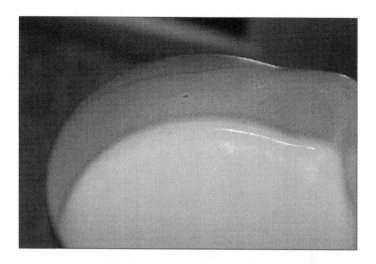

Microfoam – Perfect for latte

Macrofoam – More suited for cappuccino

I'll make the assumption you'll be using the steamer attached to your espresso machine. When dipping the tip into the milk, then provided it's inserted to the correct depth the result should be that the milk is heated and the desired foam is created.

Steamers differ from machine to machine usually by the amount of steam they omit. For this reason, it's handy to know what to look, and listen, out for because the amount of time it takes to create the foam will often vary. You'll need to use your judgement at first, and with experience, you'll soon perfect the technique. In general, however, the process should take between ten and forty seconds, quite broad, I'm sure you'll agree.

Aim to keep a happy medium between heating the milk and creating the foam. If this delicate balance tips in either direction then the end result will be inconsistent; either hot milk with little foam, or macrofoam that's not sufficiently heated.

What You Need

- Container for steaming milk, ideally stainless steel but if not then a plastic milk jug will suffice.
- Milk, either 2% or 3.25% fat is ideal.
- Thermometer (attached to steaming jug) for monitoring milk temperature.
- Espresso machine with steam wand.

Foaming Principles

First, ensure the steam wand nozzle is clean. Ideally this should be cleaned after every use.

When first turning the nozzle, the wand will omit hot water until it's hot enough to produce steam. The better machines boil the water quicker but you should still be prepared to catch any water in a spare cup until it's heated to 100 degrees Celsius.

Pour the milk into your jug. Ideally, the jug should be filled to around halfway or perhaps a bit more, taking into account that the milk will increase in volume by around 50%.

The following graphic should help explain where the foaming tip needs to be placed within the steaming jug.

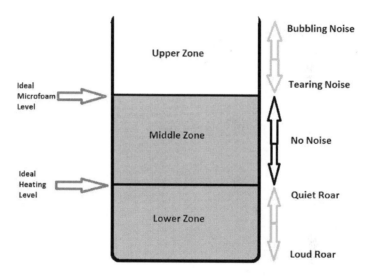

As you can see, there are three zones within the steaming jug; the upper zone, the middle zone and the lower zone. Each zone represents one-third of the jug contents and you'll need to listen for when one zone ends and another begins.

When placing the steaming nozzle within the upper zone, you will hear a loud bubbling noise, which gradually phases into a tearing noise as the nozzle sinks deeper within the milk. As you enter the middle zone then the noise should almost cease altogether. As the nozzle reaches the lower zone then you should begin to hear a quiet roar that will become gradually louder as you reach the base. Give it a try and see for yourself.

In order to create the perfect microfoam then you should position the nozzle where the upper arrow is for the duration of the process, around one third of the distance down. At this depth, the tearing sound should be quiet but you should be able to hear it. If you lower the jug, so that the nozzle is positioned higher then you'll create macrofoam more suitable for cappuccino. The difference between the two foams lie within a very small area and so you need to be careful and use your eyes, and ears especially, to ensure the correct foam for your chosen drink is created. It really can be a fine line, which is why so many of my Costa Coffee lattes are poorly made.

Remember that during the task the milk will increase in volume, a process known as stretching, which again means you must use your ears and adjust the level as you progress. It's for this purpose that you can't simply set the jug down, turn the nozzle and walk away. No, you must remain active. For latte (microfoam) then ideally you should not stretch the milk any more than 50%, however you will want to stretch it a little further for cappuccino.

Keep an eye on the thermometer attached to the steaming jug. You should aim to heat the milk to around 150 degrees Fahrenheit (65 degrees Celsius) (although 160 is fine if you like it hotter). If the steaming wand is positioned at the upper arrow for the duration, or around one-third of the way down, then it's likely the milk will foam before it reaches the required temperature. The best scenario is to arrive at the required temperature at around the same time as the milk has completed foaming. Of course, this will mean alternating between the two points (one-third down and two-thirds down) until reaching that parity. If you don't have a thermometer then the temperature of the steaming jug should be just enough to give discomfort to your hand when holding onto it. If you heat the milk above 160 degrees Fahrenheit then you risk curdling the milk and ruining the foam.

When completed, allow the finished foam to stand for a few moments. You may often witness baristas banging the finished cup down against the countertop. This is to assist gravity in allowing the heavier milk to sink to the bottom and the lighter foam to float to the top.

ESPRESSO DRINK RECIPES

Americano

This one is easy - Just add around 6 ounces or so of hot water to a shot of espresso.

Café Mocha

Pull two shots of espresso into a tall glass. Mix in chocolate syrup or powder. Add steamed milk nearly to the top. Squirt whipped cream over the milk and garnish.

Cappuccino

Pull one or two shots of espresso. Add twice as much steamed milk over the top, then add milk foam over the top of that.

You may experiment with the exact proportions if you wish. If you like you can garnish with coco.

Espresso Macchiato

Pull one or two shots of espresso. Then add milk foam over the top.

Latte

Steam about three times as much milk to espresso. Then add one or two shots of espresso to the milk.

Flat White

The flat white is closely related to the latte. However, greater care must be taken not to over foam the milk, there must be few if any bubbles in the finished product. In addition, where in latte, the espresso is added to the steamed milk, with the flat white the steamed milk is added to the espresso.

Espresso Con Panna

One shot of espresso topped with whipped cream.

Café Bonbon

One shot of espresso and pour over an equal amount of condensed milk. The mixture should stay separate until mixed.

Depth Charge / Eye Opener

One shot of espresso poured over a cup of brewed coffee.

Dead Eye

Three shots of espresso poured over a cup of brewed coffee. Perfect hangover cure.

Iced Cappuccino

One or two shots of espresso poured over ice. Add three ounces of cold milk and top with foam if desired.

Café Cubano / Cafecito

This is perhaps easier made with a Moka pot than with an actual espresso machine. Place 1 or 2 teaspoons of brown demerara sugar in your cup and boil your espresso as usual. You need to mix the first small quantity of espresso produced into the sugar until you create a brown paste. Allow the rest of your espresso to be produced by the Moka pot and pour into the paste and stir.

Cortado

Espresso mixed with an equal quantity of hot milk.

FINALLY

I hope you've enjoyed this guide and that now you'll be able to make perfect espressos, at home, the vast majority of the time. Remember that not even the most experienced baristas of Italy get it right 100% of the time. Having said that, if you follow the advice in this book you'll be making espresso better than you've ever had before and I promise you'll impress everyone at your next friend gathering.

If you've enjoyed this book and feel others may benefit from it too, then why not leave an honest review on the sales page.

Thanks.

Made in United States
Orlando, FL
10 March 2022

15633039R00028